D1484965

Not Lost Since Last Time

Jean Atkin

Oversteps Books

First published in 2013 by

Oversteps Books Ltd
6 Halwell House
South Pool
Nr Kingsbridge
Devon
TQ7 2RX
UK

www.overstepsbooks.com

Copyright © 2013 Jean Atkin
ISBN 978-1-906856-38-0

All rights reserved. No part of this book may be reproduced,
stored in a retrieval system, or transmitted in any form, or by
any means, electronic, mechanical, photocopying, recording
or otherwise, or translated into any language, without prior
written permission from Oversteps Books, except by
a reviewer who may quote brief passages in a review.

The right of Jean Atkin to be identified as the author of this
work has been asserted by her in accordance with the
Copyright, Designs and Patents Act 1988.

Printed in Great Britain by imprint digital, Devon.

for Paul, Lenny and Dougie

Acknowledgements:

Some of these poems have been published in: Acumen, Ink, And Other Poems webzine, Sweat and Tears webzine, New Writing Scotland, Northwords Now, Poetry Ireland Review, Poetry Scotland, Pushing Out The Boat, Southlight, The Eildon Tree, The New Shetlander and The Wordsworth Trust website.

Coppice won 1st prize in the Ways With Words Poetry Competition at Dartington Hall in 2008. The sequence *The Byre, The Horseman, The Letter* won 2nd prize in the Kirkpatrick Dobie Competition (University of Glasgow) 2008. *Stations of the Corpse Road, Grasmere* won joint 1st prize in the Torbay Open Poetry Competition 2009. *Not Lost Since Last Time* was runner-up in the Mirehouse Poetry Competition 2010. *The Finned Man of Rascarrel* was runner-up in the Elmet Poetry Competition 2010. *Recipe for a Crofter* won 1st prize in the Ravenglass Poetry Competition 2010. *The Children of Lir* won Second Light Live's Poem of the Month in June 2012.

The poems included in the pamphlet *Lost at Sea* (Roncadora Press 2011) were shortlisted for the Callum MacDonald Poetry Pamphlet Award that year.

Contents

Coppice

How the swifts' wings bisected the blue
above the coppice wood –
so sudden shade was first a lack
of speed and height and flight.
Our pupils dilated, our skins cooled.
Our ankles were feathered in dog's mercury.
I bent, touched sheets of stitchwort, violet, woodruff –
how they were shot with indigo, the warp and weft of bluebell.

How you relaxed, and smiled, and with your finger
smoothed the slowly easing corrugation
that was greening on a hazel leaf,
and told me how coppice cut,
and grown, and cut in every generation,
can live forever.

Species Loss

Without us, oak seedlings would press upward
through meadow grasses, compete, then shade them out.
Winter ice would pry into packed stone
and dykes, at first slowly, tumble.
Sheep would scramble out through rocky gaps,
breed, lamb late, be uncommercial.
Tarmac would furrow, small mammals weave
their desire lines in curves of bent grasses.

Under the green load of the coppice,
bluebells would starve from lack of light.
Scrub and bramble would replace them
seethe lightward into saplings.
Without our hands, our blades,
the hazels would die out at last, uncut.

Stations of the Corpse Road, Grasmere

I
They climb the Corpse Road,
burdened, breathing purple
deadnettle. They do slow
close-up of shepherd's purse

II
and gain the split slate
horizontals of walls chocked
like hymn books, locked onto gradient,
their pages loosened over tree roots

III
and a dead elm singing
and bee hum
in the fox-and-cubs
and gear change stutter on the hairpin

IV
and their eyes taste thin
furred cream of elderflower:
libation, sacred
to the memory of.

V
Though underfoot they clutch
wet emerald rock, mossed
in the old religion,
underhand, outcropped

VI
and gapped
as gaping mouths,
in search of air,
or water.

I Recipe from a Crofter

This is Bessiewalla Yow – a sheep's cheese
from the Treeless Region, which
will last you through
the end of winter and provision
the hungry gap.

Take a gallon of four day old milk
and sieve through muslin in a cold dairy.
It's bad luck to turn away strangers
while the cheese is dripping
into stoneware.
On the fifth day turn out the cheese,
and wrap in nettle leaves.
Bury the truckle for six weeks.
Choose your receptacle cautiously:
by April the rats are hungry.
Best has been a tin trunk
with luggage tags from Warsaw,
Dublin and Guernica.
The receptacle should be dug shallowly
into stony ground in rain.
Keep a count of the worms. It may be
that they're recovering.

Peel off only enough leaves
to cut the cheese
at any one time.

Eat sparingly.
Spring may be late.

II Advice Provided for Dispersed Populations

To brew a Herbal Remedy for Inexperience
and Remote Postcode, pick
Lesser Sea Spurrey off shingle
at low tide, and wilt
in a round pewter dish.
Infuse eight perforate
leaves of Cloudy Samphire and strain
in a draught of Spotted Medick
(an umbellifer naturalised now in wet woods).
Add four ounces of the hairy spikes
of Wrenbane.
Stir the whole into a quart pot
of vinegar.
Wait three days.

Drink a draught with honey
on waking, for a week.

Speak up.

The Byre

Stone pickers worked these hills,
harvested rock behind the plough,
left it mounded cold
as January drifted
in their small fields. And built

the byre out of the land.
Vast walls massed on the long bank
in drystone grip held up by weight.
Shippon, stable, bothy, barn
gathered under rainy slates. Dark

and warm with beasts, the air thick
like you could shovel it, could
breathe horse, shifting its weight,
gloss and iron on straw and cobble,
rattle of rope and block. Soaked

into the stones the scuff
of boots at the bothy's step
and scrape of fireside chairs.

The Horseman

In the dark the sleepers
under the sarking, a hold
of migrants stowed away
in the roof spaces, foreign
and seasonal, like swallows.

Rolled in his blanket, a young man
misses his girl. His arms empty,
his eyes open to first white light
seeping under slates. He thinks
how her hair shines, like horses.

A shout outside,
then men around him yawning,
stretching, swearing
at the day. He waits his turn
to fumble down the ladder

stiff fingered in the coldness
and greyness, and birdsong,
early hours ache still in his back.

The Letter

He leans into horses, brushing,
brushing, their yesterday's sweat
flicking from the bristles in rhythm
with his breath. He thinks
how their coats shine.

On the hill, the team throw
their hot weight against the earth.
The harrow bucks behind.
He calls them at the headland,
breathes their sweat as they turn.

Men clog shod on cobbles
queue for their piece
at the bothy door. They warm
segged hands on bowls.
Horses rest, hind hooves tilted.

He climbs the ladder to kneel
on his blanket. Her words
muffle the men's talk beneath.

Then folds her love letter back
between the whinstones, feels
the sarking stroke his cheek.

Glencairn Rooks

Under a cold sky slaked like lime to white morning
the feed-buckets weighting my hands,
my ears drummed with dark fanned air.
I stopped and turned up my face
to an arrowhead of birds.

Saw them wing darkness into ragged daylight
heard them conversational above our fluent roofs.
How for them Glencairn spread dizzying below
how they were focused on some destination
too plain for me to see.

Spare dark birds, they left me earth-slowed,
wrung by their raucous blare to feel a pang
for never seeing earth from a bird's share of sky

to never split that first hundred feet of tree-skim air,
or beat a line straight from hill to loch
with the purposeful flight of rooks.

Galloward, 1925

A country boy's job,
the laying out of corpses
on a winter's day.

He treads the brae upward
each snow creak step
one nearer to the dead, and evening.

His landscape is re-written
in white, the dykes smoothed over
so distances deceive.

Just now the holly keeps him right.
Higher up he sees
the oil lamp in the window –

for him, Galloward's grim
first footer, though
the peat reek reels him in.

He kicks off snow at the threshold.
The old wife lights a candle
and puts him to the stair.

The flame's waver hunchbacks him
on uneven walls. His heart pumping,
hot breath clouding the still room.

The old man, gape mouthed,
in the cold bed, his eyes jellied wide.
His sharp tongue is shrunken,

and all his hardness
waxed away. Later, the boy will tell
how his own palms sweated.

Next day, he helps to heft
the coffin to the hearse. The old wife
shuts the door.

They take him, in snow,
to the kirkyard, snow so bad,
that years on, all the boy keeps

is how he hid from the gale,
and shambled drifts in the lee
of warm plumed horses.

Galloward

Galloward grips its hollow below the ridge;
stall and hall bared to the wind,
and gables crazed by rain.
I walk twisted, cagoule
squall-rattled in my ear.

Never cut down a holly. It streams
water past dry shade, protects
from wind and witches.
I climb a gate running in rust,
wade nettles among the tattered steadings.

The front door is prone in the yard,
sneck latched to mud, and finger weathered.
I cross the threshold to a foundered house,
where slates grate under my step.
Voices called here, up the splintered stair.

For comfort, I stand on the smooth swag
of a flagstone. A window frame swings, emptied.
Out there a plough horse shifted its weight,
while a man ate his piece in the warm. A woman
chose these flowery kitchen tiles.

Ribby with laths and flaking limewash,
Galloward is holding on,
but soaked, walls frail as paper.
By the hearth its lingering folk
mere smears of damp in a mushroom season.

What happens at night

Now the lamb and I are enfolded by dark hills.
I feel his weakness, my thumb under his jaw.
He sucks at the bottle; we are flicked over by bats.

I think how the day's sun was swallowed
some time back by cloud banks and how,
below us, the lochans

are like sheets of buckled tin,
laid out between the scarps,
under slabs of moonlight.

A day ago a plane flew clean off the radar,
trued like a gannet, as if it pleated back
its wings, to spear the ocean.

From this hill the lochans float upward
into dusk. There's no wind.
Radar floods the sky. I still get
to breathe thin smells of fleece and milk.

'O you angels, who guard the people'

The house breathed like a sleeper,
just audible in doorways. Its walls exhaled
a sifting into silence.
And all the centuries hanging there
like soot in the chimney.
When I stood under it and looked up
it was a wide door to the stars
and the cold fell down on us each December.

I used to put my hands on the walls,
which were cool and chalky and bulbous.
I was skin to skin with the house
and skin to skin with the babies.
I used to listen with my fingers, flatten my palms,
cajole deep memories out of walls:
calls, cries and prayers soaked into stone.
The ghosts walking, lifting latches.

We played Hildegard von Bingen to the house
O vos angeli, qui custoditis populos –
sounds so old even this house was unquarried:
each sparse note snagged
on iron window catches.
And since we've left, our voices,
and our children's, must be suspended there
in falling lime dust.

Small Son

Holding him's a pendulum
rocking us through the small hours.
This is the time

in the dark clock-case of night
when love like shutters is closing us
in quiet rooms

where we don't talk
but learn at length
the easing-down of heart rate.

Shared air sways
between us,
in metronomic minutes.

We have pulled silence up
like a drawbridge.
His hair stops my mouth, sweetly.

Jonquières

Leaning out, I see the cold ruelle
is a plough curve fallen
between tall houses
among nine varieties of iron balcony.
This is the hour of shutters
swung back with the sound of boats
nosing a boardwalk.
The yap of a dog
locked out on a balcony
is the signal
for a new rose-sun
to slide honeyed
over thick grey pantiles.

A dented Citroen van
corrugates in reverse
before the shining windscreen
of a new bus, which pursues it
and the bus brushes
below cables that rope wall to gutter.
The cables stream blondes,
football, con-men, Fiats
into kitchens, roiling them
through steamy, fragrant coffee.

Someone's piebald tomcat is lying,
not asleep,
with his head at the wrong angle,
in the dry gutter.

Gorges de la Buège

Drought. *Sécheresse*. A silk caress of dust.
White river-bed dead still, slow drift of flies.
A lizard flickers on a stone.

We step down to this freak-show river,
wade its absence, staring through
its empty depth, its silent waterfalls.

Moss washed all one way, and stilled. Limestone
scoured to floury dust. Tree trunks greened
by the disappeared surge of a bow-wave.

Midday's silent, the songbirds must be higher,
whipping hot through the garrigue. Down here
we leap lost pools and gaze at trees

once flood-torn, now arrested in mid-air;
gripped fast, as if a camera stopped rolling
when we stumbled on the scene.

The kids are out for danger, chasing red-winged
grasshoppers. They shout over a praying mantis.
It's huge and leaf-green weird, but stunned by heat.

You and me, walking more slowly
downstream to Vareilles, where the packhorse bridge
will cross us back into the everyday.

Andalusian

Cycling into Arcos early one morning,
and just before Christmas, I saw a horse.
We'd passed orange trees growing

along the road at blue dawn, and wondered who
picked the fruit growing up from the pavements
or reached for it from balconies.

Shutters rattled upwards as we passed.
We dropped a gear to climb into the sun
that fired the white town's peak.

Someone shouted from an open door.
And in the smell of bread and the grey roar of vans
and the near-frost, I saw the horse.

Haltered, he pivoted around
his strength. The narrow yard he danced in
penned him on three sides. I rode

more slowly, recognised
the bold blood veering
through him.

Dark dappled horse with almond face,
he turned his head and eyed me
through the straight rain of his forelock.

He was trouble. He stamped
and shimmered on the concrete
in his suit of lights.

Not Lost Since Last Time

The borrowed pony, round as a rolling sea,
walks willing, for once, plodding the boom
of breakers down a sheeptrack.

Reins loose through fingers and gut jarred softly
by hooves, a child riding between leather
and sky, slack and absent, her thoughts

coiled in her grandmother's shell
on its dusty sill, in not its native land.
The shell's still curled round this green morning

when, young and sudden, a fox is on the path,
giving its absolute attention, and not afraid.
The fox, the pony, the sheeptrack,

the stones steeped in the fell below
this red-brush moment's contact
between wild, and not-wild.

The child watching and finding
that she was all of them
and not them either.

*

Still it sits like a small red god on the sheeptrack,
ears cocked. It turns up again in the ribcage,

an expanding red-brush moment's joy
at being all of them, and not them;

like holding the shell, fat weight in the hand,
and checking that the sea's inside, not lost since last time.

George Aiken's Map, 1846

As if these paper islands
were crumpled in a ball
and crushed and
hurled
into backlit rain
and rolled
before a filthy wind –

she wrings the sheet
and smoothes it
with strong palms, as if
next she'd iron these wet
and whalebacked hills -

as if a capsized gale
ripped up wet paper
and melted it to rags,
the broken coast bursts
headlong out of spray –

rain-soaked at Sumburgh
George loses his grip
on a rope –
feels the pitch
slide him, helpless,
and no longer young,
into the sea's hold.

The Knitted Roof

At Billister I lock the car.
We listen
to a constant skylark.
The bank is blued
with spring squill.
I unfold the OS map
with cold fingers.

There's something safe
about his tobacco tin
slung deep in the lee
of his jacket pocket,
tweed noost for this
small pleasure.

We follow a track
past a tin-roof byre and
an empty cottage.
The prehistoric voe
rolls on.
Out on the hill, on thin soil
below peat hags

a greener place still circled
by a tumbled dyke:
Garths, last home of the Hunters.

Flittin the peats she walks
steady, bent forward
against the kishie's weight.
Her fingers click as busily
as if she aimed to knit
her roof again in every voar.

noost: a sheltered place; kishie: a basket; voar: spring

Lost at Sea

A herring gull tears
on a roadside rabbit
at Lunabister.
Thin islands blow
like streamers off
the coast.
The custodian at Boddam
looks past me for
his view of voe
and surnames lost
at sea. Invisible
from here, in haar,
Garthsetters and Mansons,
Leasks and Mouats.
There used
to be Aikens at Ness,
Aikens at Ellister.
Once they were on Burra-Isle.

I'm reading graves at Papil.
Rub tough rain of lichen
off grey stone. 'William
Aiken who with crew
was drowned
March 12th 1866'.
I straighten up to find
the view his widow had:
the stones, the green,
the graves, the grazing
sheep. Invisible
from here, the sea
is sweeping up the voe
between the Burras.

Telescope

Dark wood polished by use and damaged
down one side, it's been
familiar to my touch since childhood.
He must have known its balance
intimately, weighed it in decisions,
fingered the fine milled edges of its eye.
All through his grainy, deck-tilt years
he shut it safe away.

I learned to tweak with a fingernail
the tiny pin on the metal shutter
which slides back to reveal
the eyepiece just as
I'm pulling on the casing, shlunck
shlunck, and this
neat cubit passes me
the vision of a sea eagle.

Far back through the glass
a wide grey sea and slant
of rain, a rig of swaying furrows,
medallions of salt, each stamped
by some small imperfection on the lens,
a whorl and ripple that lays
a long century
between my eye and his.

The Ditty Box of Thomas Gilbert Hunter Aiken

That he left Church Closs
and his mother and stowed
away on a Tyne collier
at thirteen, dodging on board
in the wash and blow
of Lerwick harbour.

That sometimes he ate
ships biscuits so maggoty they
shuffled across his plate. That he sailed
round the Horn. That he shivered
one winter on a vessel held ice-bound
for weeks in the Baltic.

That he was wrecked
in the tide-race of Ushant, rescued
by a brig bound for Cuba and dropped
at the mouth of the Tagus to row
under Torre de Belém
into white-paved Lisbon.

That in Valparaiso he
punched a man and knocked him
overboard and then
jumped in and saved him.
That he married twice but no-one
ever mentioned the first time.

That he had a strong face, a trim beard
and fierce eyebrows. His eyes look far
past my shoulder. That we know this
from a photograph. And also have his telescope,
his drawing instruments and his cut-down,
hacked-about charts table.

That he lived to see his sons survive the War
and held his grandchildren, as babies.
That his sextant and the ditty box went missing
at last, in the bombing of Liverpool
in 1940. That he never
went back to Lerwick.

Shoal

Herring,
muscle of the sea.
In all his stories,
you winked
like silver shillings
flipped
through tides.

All his life
you went by flashing
in your thousand
thousands,

ghosting
in your shoals,
like little planets
leaning
on the dark.

Janet Hunter Remembers Her Man

He said, you had to be there
in the heart-thump and stars
and see the whales rise up

black and blowing through
the herring. When the sea split
with silver and

the air leapt with water
all the glitter and livewire
of herring.

You had to be there, he said,
watching water roll
like mercury

from cautious oars, the men
whispering to the gill nets
in the bows.

He said, it was the moon,
the herring love
the moon.

Becoming Variable

i.
Attend to the gulls and forecasts heard in bed,
reassurance that we're safe from winter seas

where wrecks roll under the sea lanes, tilting
in the oily wash of ferries

or fathoms down, where whales slip freely
through the Hebrides.

ii.
You must have been there in the flap and crack of canvas
that Malin stitched for you in beads of ice

and worked a slanting Dog Watch while the gales
whipped North Utsire white at nightfall

and learned co-ordinates for the sight
of black ceramic water shattering on Rockall.

iii.
I imagine you counting, between Fair Isle
and Forties, a flock of shipwrecks,

when you slept. Long after you've gone,
I think of the course of your keel

on its barred-silver passage to the mackerel north
or on the coal road from Lerwick to Shields.

*These poems were written about my family on Shetland, and in
particular my great grandfather, who ran away to sea in 1852.*

Silent Race

Walking the tarmac
dried by frost
on the last night of January

without a torch
to see the glinting sky
ears ringing with cold

and the gale   I stopped
where the burn flows
below the road

as if its rush   and bubble
          pouring
through my short pulse

could tangle with
that silent race
of stars.

Mattie White

The Palnure burn runs over rock
and butters a slab
like a ploughman's piece.

Water melts in brown pools,
light-lit, lensing the stones.
From here the visibility's so good

I see the sunlight brimming
in all the starry pinpricks
of the river bottom.

There's nothing left in the world
but the fast clatter
of this burn after rain.

I stand around and watch reflections
waver on the granite belly
of Mattie White's Bridge.

Mattie, who's immortalised, I'm pleased
to see, on the OS map. A hoverfly
hesitates, then settles on my pen.

Parish

Gravestones are tilting into the wood,
tilting out of the kirkyard
into the dark.

They lived at Watch Tower
They lived at Wood of Cree

In the old Kirk the cobbles rise
in a thin whine, an interference
in the ears.

They lived at Black Craig
They lived at Stronord

The roof's gone and the doorways
don't have doors. But there's
still grace in a mullion.

They lived at Glenamour
They lived at West Knockbrex

Names flake from stones.
The grass is globed with droplets,
run to seed.

They lived at Auchenleck
They lived at Glenshalloch

In Holm Wood

The Minnoch dapples, fly-danced.
At noon we find a shiver on the water
suggesting stars at midnight.

Round a bend in the path we see trees
which have fallen and wrapped one another
in limbs, familiar as lovers.

Soaking wet bracken and grasses muffle this
September wood. Thin pink heather
and purple scabious light it.

Here are vast stones that stopper a dyke-end
where a dead thorn tree stands
like its own ghost, blurred with moss.

We walk and lichen flowers
on every fallen branch and acorns split
and green at every step.

We breathe in oak-air, laced
with draughts of peat and the sudden
swing of a jay.

To a Barn Builder in Cumloden Wood

You must have had plans
when you stood in the purple foxgloves,
sharpened your saw, and cut
through railway sleeper walls
to make this squinting window.

The corrugations of your roof are warmed
by early sun. The rivets in your gables
keep their grip. Your barn sags
only slightly to the left. A rush of ash
has seeded through its footings.

I peer in through a gap,
where a sleeper sags outwards
like a tooth. Inside, the silence
of people like you, who've left,
and left their tools.

A wash copper. A cast-iron range you heaved
from a farm kitchen and stored
for later. Your trowel, set neatly on a shelf.
Also an owl, which leaves suddenly
through the open doorway at the back.

The Bull Mask

They clap darkness
over his head
and someone grasps him
by the arms.
They strip him of his shirt
despite his struggle.
This is it ma lad!
He knows it is.
He breathes in leather, rank
with bull, and stumbles
but they catch him,
laugh at him,
and drive him on.

Now he sees what
the bull sees: two dim
curved worlds.
He swings his head
and now and then
a horn of daylight splinters
from the edge.
They yank the strap tighter
behind his head.
– *It's now,*
he thinks, and trembles
like a beast,
at what may come.

Is the brother a blind man?
Yes.
A chorus, a roar.
What way came you here?
Through crooks,
and crooks and straights,
as the nearest road led us.
What brought you here?

He staggers as they dig him
in the ribs. He struggles
for the words he's learned.
To find the secret.

Did you come here
of your own free will?

He's willed this.
Yes.

Hold up your right hand.
And place yourself
neither sitting, nor standing,
bowing nor bending,
naked nor clothed,
and say this after me.

Slowly they let go his arms
and still in darkness
down he goes
upon his knees.

I do most solemnly
take upon me the vows and secrets
of horsemanship.

He listens to his own voice
repeat the Word. He listens
to his heart pounding,
and sees in his bull-dim,
thunderous, the huge
red heart of a horse.

I shall always conceal
And never reveal.
I shall not cut it or carve it
paint it or print it
write it or engrave it.

They jostle him and his hair
gets trapped in the strap
as they jerk it free
and he blinks and shakes his head
and breathes the byre
and not the bull.
He sees them open all
their mouths at once and never
in his life forgets
their voices' boom
and chant that soaks
like neatsfoot
into wood-lined stalls
and dangling row of bridles.

Here's to the horse with the star on his brow
Here's to the mare with the bell on her breast
They are easy to harness
They are fleet in the yoke
It's a good going horse that works with a nod!

He's laughing now, they're knocking him
between their shoulders and
their eyes approve.

Here's to the lad that can always conceal
And keep a thing hidden!
Bring both his horses at the crack of a whip
And stand like a stone when bidden.

The bull mask lies where it fell
on the byre floor. He kicks
away its sightless eyes
and joins the men.

This poem contains words from the ritual ceremonies of the largely 19th century Society of the Horseman's Word. This secret society initiated its members in rituals which required blindfolding, and were once commonplace across Scotland. There is a fine black leather bull mask in Newton Stewart Museum.

The Night Horses

are stalled between sleep and dreaming.
In the steading they lower their massive heads
to the earth's nod. In darkness
white-faced Clydesdales lip at nothing.

Below a halo of bats they rest their load
of feather and bone and horn. They hear,
don't hear, the scrape of shoes as a gelding shunts
his weight to tilt the other hind hoof.

Their slow brains orbit the tracks and rigs
breathing in water, heather, grasses.
Sometimes through the slats above their heads
they watch the burn and tremor of the stars.

A Use for Teeth

Who made the necklace of horse's teeth?
(It lies here on museum glass, the strangest thing).

Was it a quiet man at dawn, who picked
a white jawbone from under his plough?

Or a childless woman who worked each tooth loose
from its socket and saved them in a bag?

Or the man who tore down a relic
nailed to the byre wall, because

he couldn't bear the rain that fell
from its eyeholes any longer?

Somebody imagined a torque in ivory.
They laid the teeth on a scrubbed table,

took a saddler's needle and waxed thread
and set about binding and knotting

between each tooth, with such neatness.
And then there's the surprise touch

of decorative stitching in dyed blue string
that stripes the plain thread. Was it love?

To be certain, somebody took it in their hands,
and stood before a mirror,

and tried it on.

*A 'Necklace of Horse's Teeth' is on display in Newton Stewart Museum,
provenance unknown.*

The Lunkie Hole

It was easy, the green voluminous
bracken on the hill, then granite nudged
my boots, and now and then a harebell.

The sun grew old and hot on my back.
I tried to keep to the path, but it was part-time burn,
and rose and sank in the peat.

By Gairland the day had turned sticky. I felt sweat
spring. The air sank hammocked between
the peat-stained, myrtle-scented hills.

Higher, the map marked a ford where once sheep
leapt and struggled on the stones. I rested
where they drove them through and up the lip

and on to Rig of the Jarkness and the loch.
But now the burn's run wild, with coursing boulders
wall-eyed all the way, and not a sheep for miles.

Dragonflies surged around my knees, skilled
in the present of their two-moon lives. Slowly
I climbed peat moss riddled through with water.

Then rain came, and a net of midges on the loch
and I watched where a boulder clear of the water
stood for centuries and never felt the cold.

And at Low Cornarroch I found a threshold stone.
And then the hearth, and then a hird's mouth breathing out
through the lunkie hole in the sheep ree.

Hird: a shepherd
Lunkie hole: a passageway built through a stone wall to allow
sheep to pass through
Sheep ree: a sheepfold built of drystone walls in the Galloway Forest

Universe

What's constant?
Not one stone.
Starlight pours
through wallheads.
At the end of mortar,
dust.

What's current?
Not one breath.
Light falls and falls
at the end of stars.
We run but we can't
catch up.

The Absence of Sheep

It's intricate, this sheep ree, links and passageways
to fox them. The sheep, like water,

run down the face of Mullwhachar to pour
between the rock walls of the Buchan Burn.

Down here the smell of lanolin and panic, the Blackface
tricked by grinning dogs, who leave

no choices and no dodging back. And the dykes,
raddled then, with shearing dags and blood.

It could have been some other year's cold August.
I might have walked here by the sheep ree

in last light bleat and settle of the flock
and waited for a man from Glenhead.

I might have stood here in the moss, with seedling birch,
and learned to take life sturdily, and short.

Glenhead

The track continues between byres,
some roofed, some not.
A metal gate rusts, but would
keep stock out of the orchard,
if there were any.
Trees overlean, drop tiny apples.

They're working back to wild.
The orchard's pathless, just
the slightest press of grasses
where a fox passed, cider-bellied,
in the early dark.
I eat an apple, sweet, red-blushed.

June 1900, and a traveller wrote
of his welcome here – a straw hat lying
on the garden path, a cool parlour,
a shelf of books. Now bracken
has taken Glenhead's garden. I touch
the ashlared granite of the windowsill

and then I touch raw breezeblock
mortared where the panes should be.
The same for every window, every door.
In every room, the dark's walled in.

Names Spoken in Kirk

A grainy dark is falling on the stones.
There are no beams, but the roof
is beamed with constellations.

Tonight the stars and cobbles purr as if
they remembered older words. *Lord, thou hast been
our refuge from one generation to another.*

I name some names. *Christina Meikle Starke.
Wilhelmina Mason. Agnes Margaret Murray.*
Their slabs recline against the walls.

*Lord, thou hast been our refuge from one doorway
to another.* Their dates are vague and flaking.
I may have read them wrong.

But I sense the mudstains on their hems,
their hardworked hands and narrow backs
on benches down the dimming nave.

And by the light of elder stars
I know the people of this kirk
have slipped their names.

O constellations hear our prayer.
There's no wood in this kirk any more.
It eyes the sky. It's purely stones and air.

*Names Spoken in Kirk contains language from The Scottish Book of
Common Prayer.*

The Dark Farms

And now they're emptied
      the dark farms
      now crouched in their earths.

For years
they swallowed glints
      and flakes of stars
      as mica shines in granite.

Now cloud hangs in veils
          there's no hill
          there's no moon

only rain-soaked wool

            as sheep
            press into the cottage
       find their shelter
       under the lum.

Lum: fireplace with stone and cob chimney breast

Murmuration

The starlings lean
like woodsmoke on the fields,
and blow away.

Bedded in leaves the Wood of Cree
aches in the gale
and sleepwalks into winter.

Rain maps the hills.
Our roaming thoughts
drain down to silt.

The house is filled with hollow coats.
The mice climb in the walls,
familiar ghosts.

The starlings start to tilt,
they make an end, pull out their stitches,
fold, descend.

What's Common

Under the gigantic waver of the stars, we sit
on the reeling hill to be reminded of our Earth,
which happens twice.

First in the mapping, and the act of framing details,
which stand for ways and places
we've never been and never will

and second, in what's common, waited for, and missed:
the smell of small children; the paperiness of onions;
the last brief hesitation – and the kiss.

What's Human

Outside under
this field of stars
in a frost   that slows
the blood

we are the dark.

We hold in a creel
of air
what's human

and stretch out
our fingertips
to the whorl   of galaxies

to feel for what's not there.

*These poems were written about the Galloway Forest, its dark
skies, its ruins and its farming community.*

The Children of Lir

His hands were folded. He seemed
to be waiting. I saw him lower
his eyes to earth

as I landed, a brother at each wing tip.
Behind us the sea lough tolled with the bell.
When it had stopped, he spoke.

I remember the coarseness of his robe,
his mudstained feet. His voice was narrow
as reeds. Rain fell.

We heard him out.
I searched my brothers' eyes: and then
we spread our wings. I felt the loosening

of flight feathers, saw them fall;
I watched smooth plumage snow
from thinning bones.

I folded, for the first time, shriven fingers
and with my stranger's hand I touched – and found
skin slack on flesh and desert dry.

My hair curved round me
long and faint and grey.
White down fanned to ground.

Shameless, my favourite brother stood
and stared into the sky. I saw him lank
and naked.

His eyes filled. I took his hand.

The monk prayed. Rain fell.

The Finned Man of Rascarrel

He claimed his father heard it
from his wife's father, the tale
of the day the finned man
beached himself
on the shore at Rascarrel.

At neap tide each May he liked to tell
how a child came shrieking
to the haaf nets to fetch the men;
and the way they took a shovel,
new sharpened just that morning.

How they went, and stood around him
in a circle, taking in
his colour, and the way the skinny
dorsal down his back
rose and fell
with his breathing.

How when they asked his name
and business, he made some sound
they took to be a hunting cry of whales.
But they knew his cursing solid

as the splay of limpets;
and when he shouted
they said his salt tongue broke
on the rocks
and fell back hissing
through the shingle.

They put the shovel by.

And then they rolled him
over and over
wading together
into deep water.

Blodeuwedd

A woman in a caul of owls
walks feather-naked in the dark.

She hunts the oakwoods,
sings below her breath.

She's pliable
as saplings.

At every stride the owls' eyes ripple
with her moony flesh

and round her they rotate
their hungry heads

and snap their beaks so field-voles bolt
and freeze.

She cannot stop. She cannot feel
the thorns. Benighted she

cannot recall the golden broom
and meadowsweet of day.

How to Become a Bird

First choose a tree. The kind
you feel you could climb. Or hug.
It should be spring: the leaves damp,
unfastening; sap thudding in the xylem.

Place your foot in the crook
of a low branch. Then pull up
and feel your earthly weight. Too late
to waver now. The leaves
are filtering the sky.

Look up, not down. Be still. Notice
everything about the air. How it wraps you.
The blue and blow of it. How the tree
strains for it. How your feathers tension it.

As you'd expect, the trunk will fork,
go on dividing. The tree's green skin
climbs skywards. This time of year, it never
rests. You'll find it easier to get a grip
with claws. Learn

to check. Turn the bead of your eye
to be sure of an absence of cats. Becoming prey
your fear will start to rattle you
like twigs. Your bones will grow full
of light as candled eggs.

And then you'll flutter out
onto the crown, disturbing only
a veil of moths, and other things
to eat. Beat your wings.
Be gone.

Oversteps has previously published books by the following poets: David Grubb, Giles Goodland, Alex Smith, Will Daunt, Patricia Bishop, Christopher Cook, Jan Farquarson, Charles Hadfield, Mandy Pannett, Doris Hulme, James Cole, Helen Kitson, Bill Headdon, Avril Bruton, Marianne Larsen, Anne Lewis-Smith, Mary Maher, Genista Lewes, Miriam Darlington, Anne Born, Glen Phillips, Rebecca Gethin, W H Petty, Melanie Penycate, Andrew Nightingale, Caroline Carver, John Stuart, Ann Segrave, Rose Cook, Jenny Hope, Christopher North, Hilary Elfick, Jennie Osborne, Elisabeth Rowe, Anne Stewart, Oz Hardwick, Angela Stoner, Terry Gifford, Michael Swan, Denise Bennett, Maggie Butt, Anthony Watts, Joan McGavin, Robert Stein, Graham High, Ross Cogan, Ann Kelley, A C Clarke, Diane Tang, Susan Taylor, R V Bailey, Alwyn Marriage, John Daniel, Rebecca Bilkau, Simon Williams and Kathleen Kummer.

For details of all these books, information about Oversteps and up-to-date news, please look at our website:
www.overstepsbooks.com